Visions IN Verse™

poetry and art that bring tears to the eyes and joy to the heart

by Ruth Kuttler

poet, author, graphic artist

Published by
Divinely Inspired Books
Naples, Florida

Divinely Inspired Books
Naples, Florida
www.visionsinverse.com

Second Edition, Divinely Inspired Books, 2005

Designed and Illustrated by Ruth Kuttler
Cover Design by Tami Dickson of Tami Dickson Creative
Book Layout by Kelly Hall
Edited by Peter Tomassi

Library of Congress Control Number: 2005903721

ISBN 0-9715580-1-9

Dedication

This collection of poetry is dedicated to those special people in my life who supported my burning desire to live my passion, let go of fear and bring my dream to fruition. First and foremost, special thanks to my husband Paul Kuttler for his support and encouragement, and never complaining about the expense and the lost income from not "getting a real job." I also owe my mother Mollie Gisser many thanks for expanding my vision to share this poetry and art with people everywhere. I am grateful to Jeannette Boucher, my guardian angel who saw more in me than I saw in myself at a time when I most needed someone to believe in me. Mostly, I am grateful to my creator for endowing me with the gifts and wisdom to know my true path and purpose, and to follow my dream.

I'd be remiss if I failed to mention my readers. I dedicate this book to each man, woman or child who takes at least one thought or idea from this collection and makes a positive change in his or her life because of it–I salute and congratulate you!

Mission

Visions in Verse™ is a collection of heartfelt poems, quotes, and stories that you will love to read over and over. It consists of three sections: Inspirations, Personal Growth and Relationships.

Timeless poems and writings in the Inspirations and Personal Growth sections will help you to understand that happiness and fulfillment result from the decisions each of us chooses to make in our lives. These rhythmical verses will inspire and empower you. Mostly, they will grant you permission to think differently and become aware of self-limiting beliefs and factors in your life that may be keeping you from being where you want to be. As you read them, think about possibilities for being, doing and having the life you really want. Thinking and dreaming is the first step toward making it happen.

The Relationships Section is filled with special occasion, heartfelt sentiments and inspirational messages. Many of these poems have been illustrated and are available for purchase as framed artwork. These also include a complimentary copy of the book Visions in Verse. Please visit www.VisionsinVerse.com to view the collection and order online.

Believe in yourself for you have magic inside you.
It is not in just some of us. It is in all of us.
Most people have learned to suppress it—through
conditioning, they accept mediocrity and settle
for much less than they deserve.

Listen to your heart and you will find your magic.
You will know it through that intuitive voice that fills you
with joy and passion when it occupies your thoughts.
Find your magic and live your dreams.
When you do, your life will take amazing turns
for the better as you discover meaning,
happiness and inner peace.

Table of Contents

Inspirations

Personal Growth

Table of Contents

Relationships

Inspirations

Take time to go inside.
Settle back with eyes closed and
free your mind of thoughts and worries.
When you do this, the magnificence of God's perfect plan
will move into your conscious world.
In the stillness and quietness, you will find
all the answers that you seek.

My Daily Prayer

Bless me today, oh God . . .

Give me your blessings this day and help me to manifest your greatness beyond the realm of my human experience.

Help me to know that I am worthy, that no past transgression bars me from the gates to prosperity, joy and inner peace.

Inspire me to see challenges in my life as vehicles for expansion to a higher purpose and to know that purpose through burning passions that are always for the greater good.

Guide me to avert temptation to regress to status quo, and to rise above mediocrity beyond those limits that my consciousness defines.

Empower me to be a candle, lighting the way for others through word and deed.

Allow me to recognize opportunities and let go of fears that thwart change toward my greater good.

Grant me the wisdom to know truth and to explore and question the validity of beliefs handed down through time.

Assist me in letting go that which controls and limits my experiences.

Replenish my faith that your blessings will be answered through my prayers each and every day.

Bless me today, oh God.

The Rose

Why does the rose become a rose?
It just knows to be a rose
And not a tulip, plant or tree,
Canary, ant or bumblebee.
The oak, it knows what it's to be–
Not banyan, spruce or maple tree.
The fruit it bears, a squirrel's feast–
Not so for man or other beast.
Why are fins on fish and whales
And not on owls and cottontails?
If birds were launched without their wings
And bees and wasps without their stings,
How different would our world become
For all God's creatures, not just some.
How does a monarch know to fly?
It's born to know, to do or die.
Unlike the spider, deer or cat
It's programmed to begin like that.
It's why your eyes are not your nose,
Your ears or elbows, feet or toes.
Every atom, every space,
From scorpion to human race,
A perfect plan in perfect time
Like harmony and flawless rhyme,
A symphony of nature's glory–
God directs the sounds and story.
Why does the rose become a rose?
To be a rose is all it knows.
Divine creations, each are we–
It's why you're you and why I'm me.

The Box

Like a little China doll, so innocent and pure,
Cascading curls in ponytails, a golden brown they were.
A dazzling smile and eyes so blue they took your breath away,
This tiny child exuded love on each and every day.

In three short years, this little girl so rarely shed a tear.
She seldom asked for anything, turned sadness into cheer.
Her mom and dad had long since passed and family there were none,
Except her grandpa, stiff and cross–who never was much fun.

A mound of tape was in her hand, a trail left on the floor.
A burly man with graying hair was standing at the door.
He scolded and he lectured her, looked sternly in her eyes;
And yet she smiled, exclaimed with pride, "It's for a big surprise."

Her grandpa, he felt foolish now, but wouldn't let it show.
He walked away a little sad, she didn't seem to know.
She pushed a chair and stood on toes to reach a shelf up high.
A great big box with wrap and bows, to get it she must try.

Suddenly the box came down, crashing on the floor.
She thought she'd see her grandpa's face, instead she heard his snore.
The papers, bright and colorful, were scattered all around–
With task at hand she went to work and didn't make a sound.

When at last the work was done, admiring it with pride,
A golden box with purple bow; she found a place to hide.
On both her arms his hands of steel propelled her to the air,
Despite her tender loving face, she met a hostile glare.

(continued on page 7)

His reprimand was harsh indeed, his angry tone and words,
The mess she made and all the waste, repeatedly she heard.
After all was said and done, she looked a little blue.
She brought to him the wrapped-up box and said, "This is for you."

He wished that he could take it back, the unkind words he said.
He picked her up and kissed her cheek, then stroked her tiny head.
With care the wrappings were removed, she watched with pure delight,
As yards of tape were peeled away that bound that package tight.

The box was filled with only air; again his temper flared.
"You've given me an empty box," he angrily declared.
With sweetness and sincerity the words she spoke were true.
"This box is filled with kisses that I blew in there for you."

"Anytime you're feeling sad or need a little cheer,
Just open up this box–and you will find a kiss in here."
A lesson did he learn that day; it lasted till he died.
He learned to let her joy and love replace the rage inside.

That box he kept it all his life atop his chest of drawers.
And sometimes he would open it, remembering once more–
That tiny little three year old, so youthful yet so wise,
Who knew that kisses in a box could open up his eyes.

Angels show up in our lives in mysterious ways.
They may come to us in our sleep,
during times of silence and prayer—
or in moments of great challenge.
If we open the door, they will guide and protect us.
They offer great lessons that touch our hearts
and move our souls.

The Stranger

Wearily and still she sits, the seat as hard as stone.
Around her people young and old, yet she is all alone.
Flawless features sleek and smooth that camouflage so well
Her agony and loss of power make life a living Hell.

Idle chatter loudly droning, bags left everywhere.
Takeoff planned for half an hour with not an empty chair.
Every sound and every movement stir and agitate
Her broken body, mind and spirit merged to be her fate.

For a moment all is quiet, an image crystal clear,
Some words of hope, a warm embrace–her mother's presence near.
Soon trips home will be too hard, the magic turns to dread
As pain reminds her graphically, her future's bleak ahead.

Flight 302 is boarding now, she startles from the blare.
And from the corner of her eye, she's caught a stranger's stare.
Emaciated is his frame, his stature frail and weak,
Balanced only by a cane–a horror and a freak.

As she walks the ramp to board and searches for her chair,
Seat A-14 right next to her, the stranger's sitting there.
The look she has, a million words that show upon her face,
As shock subsides, her guilt and shame are there to take its place.

She meets his smile and shares her name–like him she'll be polite.
She hopes that he won't talk too much aboard their two-hour flight.
This fragile man without a prayer, she can't believe her ears.
With every breath he loves his life, a passion that he shares.

(continued on page 10)

Not a grimace or complaint, amazing is his way,
A final trip to say goodbye; he's grateful for each day.
She contemplates this man with awe–the message in his cheer.
Why has he come to cross her path; why is it that he's here?

No accident, coincidence, beyond deformity
His strength and will and attitude–a gift from God is he.
Her suffering she thinks about, embarrassed now to tell.
Her blessings flash before her eyes; she needn't stay in Hell.

As she shifts her paradigm, the sun displaces rain.
She sees her passions come alive and hardly feels the pain.
She leaves her seat to freshen up; she goes to comb her hair.
Intends to thank him for his gift, but finds an empty chair.

No trace of him is anywhere; could she have lost her mind?
And frantically she calls his name–no stranger there to find.
The flight attendant seems quite sure, no passenger that day,
Seat A-14 right next to her was empty all the way.

She settles back against her seat, a whisper in her ear.
"I'm in your heart, just look for me; you'll always find me here."
A choice is made for hope and dreams, from darkness comes the light.
A life forever changed that day aboard that two-hour flight.

Home

A young and lovely newlywed, a soldier by her side,
Departing for a distant land without his cherished bride.
This desert place where he would be, so primitive and bare,
With howling winds and storms of sand and only natives there.
No place was this to take a wife, he'd miss her terribly.
But she refused to stay behind; she'd go where he would be.
A tribal village near the bunker came to be their home,
And all day long she waited there, afraid and all alone.
They slept in huts of grass and twigs; no comforts were around,
With chanting tones and rituals, the only human sound.
At times his unit was deployed for days, sometimes a week,
No arms enfolding her at night, no loving words to speak.
A letter telling of her plight and plans to leave this place;
Her mother's words came back to her, "Beware–don't act in haste.
For you can be a prisoner and look upon steel bars—
Or choose to see between the lines and gaze upon the stars."
Those words replayed within her mind, their message crystal clear.
The choice was hers to live in Hell or find the joy right here.
Among the wind, the blazing sun, a stranger all alone,
A paradise for natives there, the only home they'd known.
She mingled with that native tribe and got to know their ways.
She learned to weave and speak their tongue; their light then filled her days.
And from her wisdom, gifts she shared, the natives too were blessed.
And joy and love displaced the void as she became her best.
That tribe it never was the same and neither would she be.
As each became a source of light, emerged tranquility.
Throughout her life she moved about to strange and foreign lands.
But where she was her light would shine with smile and outstretched hands.
As strangers turned into her friends wherever she would roam,
She learned that where her heart would lead, she'd always find her home.

Eternal Love

It starts out with a tender kiss, an intimate embrace.
And soon they're walking down the aisle; she's dressed in all white lace.
As they take that road through time to make a brand new start,
He takes her hand and she takes his; each promises their heart.

The passion fueling all they feel; a friendship grows so deep,
Their love is unconditional, a lifetime vowed to keep.
Time goes by, with kids and work; they're busy every hour.
The hectic days are happy ones; their passion is their power.

One night like any other night, they sleep without a sound,
And while he lies within her arms, the angels come around.
Now memories of their special love preoccupy her thoughts.
She's told her grief will pass with time, but still she is distraught.

She knows no one will take his place, be dear to her as he.
And with his spirit she is bound throughout eternity.
Years have passed and yet she dwells on days from long ago.
She still recounts their perfect life; her grief she can't let go.

Her family says, "You must go on and live your life again.
Living in the here and now will heal you, if you can."
She cries herself to sleep at night, alone sometimes so scared.
It's time to fill the empty void; she's finally prepared.

And so she comes to terms with what she knows she has to do.
A look ahead at future years, remembering what she knew.
She knows her life will never be just like it was back then,
But she's survived the pain with time and she will love again.

The Best Christmas Gift

A candle, some holly–and lights everywhere.
The season of Christmas reminds us to care.
A time to remember the ones most in need
And show them a kindness in gifts or in deed.
But the essence of Christmas should last the year through
In the words that we say and the things that we do.
The best Christmas gifts do not come in a box,
Not the tangible items like jewelry and socks.
They come from our heart when we reach out our hand
To help one another wherever we stand.
It's compassion and loving both strangers and kin,
Not about being right or compulsion to win.
What it means is forgiving enraged on the roads
And respecting all creatures from dolphins to toads.
To cherish, protect what is sometimes unseen,
Like commitment to leaving the earth fresh and clean.
It's walking the talk when we do what we say
And making a difference each in our own way.
That angel that's resting on top of the tree
Is sending her cheer and a message to be–
The peace that we wish for; I'll make it my way,
The best Christmas gift I can give you today.

Illusions

Somewhere in the thorns are the buds for a beautiful rose.
From lifeless and dead in the spring it emerges and grows.
Believe with your senses, you'll lose,
Intentions and words will confuse.
But there among promises,
Truth shows in deeds paid as dues.
Did you know...

Illusions play tricks on your mind.
Believe as you will you may find–
That diamonds aren't diamonds
But grains in the sand that will shine.
Then they're gone.
For richness is not where you stand,
Your home, your possessions or land.
It's there in your smile, in your heart,
When you reach out your hand.

Beware of the peacock that shows his true colors then crows.
He proudly approaches and sheds his fine colors and goes.
What you cannot see may surprise.
What you know to be real may be lies.
And clovers a goldmine to
See with your heart not your eyes.
Did you know...

Illusions play tricks on your mind.
Believe as you will you may find–
That diamonds aren't diamonds
But grains in the sand that will shine.
Then they're gone.
For richness is not where you stand,
Your home, your possessions or land.
It's there in your smile, in your heart,
When you reach out your hand.

Surround yourself with
positive people, thoughts and ideas.
Whatever you think about,
you attract to yourself like a magnet.
Whatever you do comes back to you—good and bad.
If you want good to come, think and do good.
Whatever you create in your mind you will manifest.
Create the life you want in your mind and visualize it every day.
Soon it will become your reality.

Go Fly Away

A stranger once he was to me,
A face without a name.
But then our paths crossed one fine day
And nothing stayed the same.
As different as the night from day
In many ways we'd be.
And yet he sparked my drive and will
That was to set me free.

A baby bird without its wings
And needing total care,
That's how I was when we first met,
So powerless and scared.
And like a mother bird he was,
I watched him all the while,
His helping ways, inspiring words,
Enthusiastic style.

Always there to pick me up
When doubts would come my way,
With kindness and encouragement
On task then I would stay.
Then one day he said to me
It's time to fly away.
And you'll be great, you've learned from me
Just what to do and say.

Go fly away, go fly away,
Go out there on your own.
These words he said I still recall,
You'll never be alone.
Go fly away, go fly away,
There's nothing you can't do.
If you believe it, it will be,
It all depends on you.

Choose to be happy and you will be.
Choose to be sad and you will be.
Life is filled with challenges.
Dwell on the negative and you will attract more of it to you.
Napoleon Hill said that
"every adversity has an equal and equivalent benefit."
Find the silver lining in each adversity and
you will find inner peace.

Emotions

The essence of humanity, the spirit of our soul;
The dance and spark of life itself, emotions make us whole.
Where joy resides and hopes abounds and love is there to find,
There sorrow rests and gloom is found as seeds within the mind.

What fires your heart with sadness, rage and makes you lose control,
It makes me laugh, explode with joy and satisfies me so.
It's why you're you and why I'm me; why black and white and gray
Are merely warped perspectives that will fade and go away.

A loved one's gone, a job is lost, a close friend moves away;
The highs and lows that come and go; these change with each new day.
While one embraces change with hope and opportunity,
Another thrives on misery and things that cannot be.

Same old records played again like fossils set in stone,
The waltz we dance with box-like moves defines our comfort zone.
Where thoughts of good alone emerge, is where our love can grow,
And nurture seeds for health and wealth; abundantly they flow.

The past is past, each moment now, a choice for us to make,
To see the beauty everywhere with inner peace at stake.
Emotions fuel our fantasies and where they are to show,
Emerges hope, desire and will to change the world we know.

My Home

This tropical environment, a land so new to me,
Is something of a paradise, just where I've longed to be.
An answer to my hopes and prayers, my expectations met,
A fantasy, a dream come true where I have no regret.

Predictable for months on end and nearly every day,
From blackened skies a downpour starts, then briskly goes away.
The air once warm and steamy now begins to dissipate.
A gentle breeze that cools the air, I find is worth the wait.

I walk on sandy beaches where I hardly have a care.
Cocoa palms sway in the breeze with seagulls everywhere.
The water in the Gulf is warm, a gentle surf on shore.
Elation felt within my heart is mine for evermore.

Here I'll remain where I belong until my days are done,
No sacrifice or change too great to bring me where I've come.
The life I've known, the past I've lived, ahead so much to do–
I love this place where I feel whole and I can start anew.

This Wooded Path

As I walk this wooded path
I'm in awe of the splendor and perfection within and around me.
In many lifetimes I've walked this very path.
I can go here whenever I choose.
In the stillness I arrive and find God in every molecule of every space.
Peace and joy fill me up, elate me and
Lift my spirits to a higher place where limits and boundaries don't exist,
Where all is possible and beautiful and good and perfect and
All the universe is connected in this oneness.
In this place I go, I see my greatness and your greatness and the
Perfection that is all there is forevermore.
In the stillness and quietness, my brothers and sisters walk there too,
I come to remember the truth, the reality of what is,
The illusion of you and me.
And I know there is only we
As I walk this wooded path.

Personal Growth

Believe in yourself.
We all have greatness within us.
Abundance and opportunities exist all around us.
Be open to receiving the good that exists
and then turn it into action.

Opening Doors

The fairer sex is what she's called, a struggle to begin.
For in a world where man is king, it's difficult to win.
But tenderness and nurturing are not to be misread,
A strength and power to rule the world lie in her pretty head.

Sometimes her magic's camouflaged, she doesn't know it's there.
Caught up in daily mindless tasks, to dream she doesn't dare.
Adversities and challenges are always in her way,
And yet she knows it's possible to change her life one day.

Every stone she stumbles on and every time she falls,
It puts her where she's meant to be—appears like blocks and walls.
And yet it is another door in spite of what it seems,
A lesson waiting to be learned, a gateway to her dreams.

Sometimes she must remind herself, the sun comes up each day.
And even in the darkest night the moon will light her way.
No rainbow comes without the storm and peace may come with wars.
Yet in her heart she knows she'll win if she keeps opening doors.

Know what you want.
Have a dream—a goal
that you can be passionate about.
Make your goal big—so big
that you could not possibly reach it as
the person you are today.
Your goal should make you stretch and grow
into the person who is capable of achieving it.

Going Not Where I Know

A ray of sun emerges, delivering dawn's new day.
Eyelids heavy strain to open while in my bed I lay.
Thinking of the life I've known, the challenges I have faced,
Successes that I thought were mine were finalized in haste.

Routines I've come to master in these middle years I fear
Are all that's left but empty dreams–a fate that's hard to bear.
Questions pondered in years long passed of who I'm meant to be.
What shall I do? Where shall I go? What is my destiny?

The strength and courage conveyed by time, instilled within my soul,
Implants the confidence that I need to once again feel whole.
I travel many roads in a quest to find my way.
So many paths from which to choose–shall I go on or stay?

Ambivalence can cloud the mind, immobilize with fear.
But not to change is not to gain, yet some they do not care.
Had pioneers not risked and tried, the progress of our time,
Would be a mere illusive dream, but dreamers were sublime.

So now the time has come I see, to make a brand new start.
And hopes and prayers will guide me while I listen to my heart.
A million thoughts of plans to make are racing through my head.
But for now, I'll stretch and smile and rise out of my bed.

Face your fears and conquer them.
Fear is a monster that dwells within all of us.
It robs us of our dreams.
Fears are like shackles.
Fear of failure, fear of looking foolish,
fear of ridicule, fear of rejection—all paralyze
and keep us from moving forward.

It takes courage to let go of fear and focus.
We must focus on what we have—skills, experiences,
wisdom, relationships, mentors, etc.
Know that on the other side of those fears are our dreams.
Perhaps your dream is freedom—freedom to realize
potential, to live happily, to define our own destiny,
or simply to live with inner peace.
Freedom lives on the other side of our fear.

Beginning Again

Through birth we each begin our life so innocent and pure.
Unique and special as we are, our future so unsure.
Seeds of greatness lie untapped in each and every soul.
In dreams we know magnificence; in life we're less than whole.

Embarking on the journey that's expected as we grow;
It's like a wheel that spins and spins, the rules we come to know.
We go through life without much thought, our dreams become obscure.
Existing superficially, we seldom search for more.

Then one morning we awake and find our world has changed.
Turbulence displaces peace, the familiar now estranged.
No compass on the open seas; we're swallowed by the gale,
Until the answer comes through prayer and calmly we set sail.

An inner strength, a sense of self begins to come alive.
Potential that we have from birth to reach we now will strive.
And never will existence be an end unto itself.
For now we know just who we are; this wisdom is our wealth.

A Better Me

The same old world that I live in, from dusk to dawn I see.
Although the same in many ways, it's changing so for me.
For when I open up my eyes to start anew each day,
A better me I've learned to be, this way that I will stay.

The me I see reflected back, an image crystal clear;
The me I've wanted so to be, is starting to appear.
I've learned to stop and look and see and listen, not just hear.
And tell my loved ones every day how much I hold them dear.

Perceptions that I once held true, that made me feel so sad,
I've learned are part of attitude, an outlook bleak and bad.
Those thoughts no longer part of me, forever gone away,
Replaced by knowing that I can, each moment of the day.

We often act but do not think, our passions are obscure;
We pay our bills and have some fun and seldom ask for more.
Convinced we do the best we can, we want just what we need,
Believe that we are limited–not destined to succeed.

Now I know this isn't so, it truly is a choice.
It all depends on turning off and tuning in a voice.
A voice that says you can, you will, you'll be the best by far.
And you'll commit to what it takes, how prosperous you are.

A better me is here to stay; I like the way I feel.
It won't be long until my dreams are turned to something real.
My pocketbook may not be now just bursting at the seam,
But wealthier I am by far, I've learned again to dream.

The Awakening

A little girl with ruffles, curls
And bobby socks I see,
A little girl with dreams so real
She knows they are to be.
Fairytales she knows by heart,
Performs with pantomime;
A knight in armor will arrive
And rescue her in time.
A royal princess she will be
And when her ship sets sail,
Her prince will hold her in his arms
And triumph will prevail.

That little girl, she now has grown,
That paradigm long gone.
The Ferris wheel she rides each day
Directs her each new dawn.
Her dreams are faded memories
Locked up behind a door.
"Is there a grander plan?" she asks,
"A purpose? Something more?"
Consumed by waves of fear and doubt
With dread and sadness too;
She knows she can't go on like this
But knows not what to do.

Just like that little girl I saw,
A new girl–now I see.
Exuberant and full of pride,
Reflecting back, she's me.
The clothes have changed just like the times,
The music, toys and school.
But dreams and hopes and fantasies
Still burning as a rule:
Awakened is that inner child
Her passions come alive.
She's buckled in the driver's seat
And revved up for the drive.

*Find a team that will cheer you on
and support your dream.
Stay away from dream-stealers—even those
well-meaning friends and family who seem to
have your best interests at heart.
They don't want to see you get hurt or fail
so they convince you not to venture—not to risk.
Listen to them and you will remain
right where you are right now.
Surround yourself with people who support your dream
and you will create the life you really want.*

The Vision

I look beyond what I don't know.
I look beyond what I can't do.
Align myself with those who can–
No boundaries then, no limits too.

I can see what others can't.
I can do what others don't.
I'll ride the gentle wave of change.
Where I succeed, most others won't.

When you set your goal, take one step at a time.
If you think about all the things
that go into climbing to the top of your mountain,
your thoughts may overwhelm you.
They may lead to negative self-talk and quitting.
Think about the value of each step as you take it.
In the end, it will be one step that puts you on your mountaintop.

This one step may come after hundreds or thousands of steps
over a period of days, weeks, months or even years.
It may come only after you have overcome struggles,
failures, rejections and many other challenges.
But the value of each step will help you to do,
to be and to have what you really want.
Perhaps it is to be free of stress and worry,
to be confident, happy and at peace.

And as you shine your light on the top of your mountain,
you will give others permission to shine theirs.
Keep your eye on your goal always, but take one step at a time.

Vicarious Living

Seeing through the eyes of others is not to see.
To live vicariously is to stand on the sidelines of life,
Never to taste of its sweetness, to feel its fullness
Or to know the true joy that it abundantly delivers.

Hearing through the ears of others is not to hear.
Acceptance of doctrines, opinions, words of wisdom
Without knowing their origin, their context–
And without experiencing their meaning,
Is perhaps to live a lie–
To leave the soul unsettled
In disharmony, empty and void.

To experience the journey of life by what others value and believe
Is not to experience life.
It is through others' interpretations or misinterpretations
That blind followers are born–
Where creativity stagnates and
Seeds of greatness multiply in
Reservoirs of untapped potential.

When truth comes through the experience of living life,
Joy and inner peace come with it,
And the realization that we are all
Magnificent creations of God.

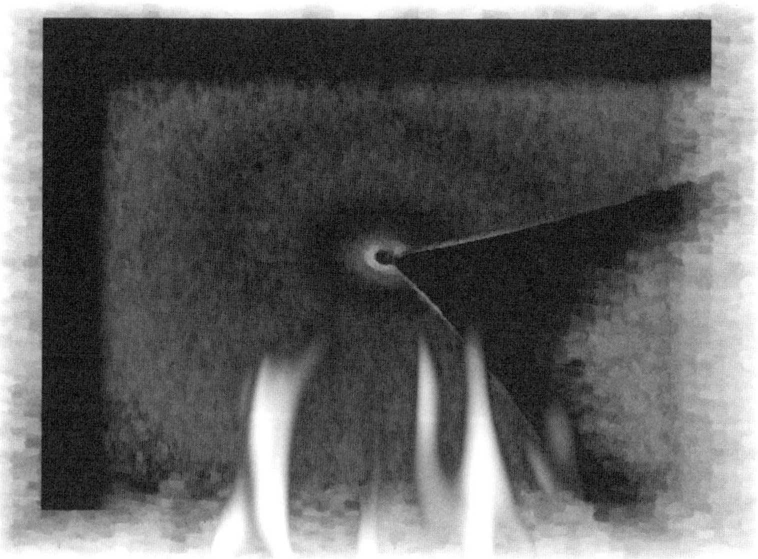

Paradigm Shift

For those of us with open minds
That blossom like a flower,
We look and listen, see and hear;
With learning comes our power.
The information we collect,
Take time to sort and sift:
When truth outweighs conditioning
Our paradigm will shift.

Our habits guiding things we do,
Beliefs we hold as true,
Programmed automatically,
To discard what is new.
Tradition plays a major role:
It's always done that way,
Philosophized as right and just;
The way that it must stay.

And in a moment's time sometimes
We find ourselves confused.
Perceptions of reality,
Distorting all our views.
Along with shift in paradigm,
A course is set to win.
Courageously we'll never go
Back where we just have been.

Don't settle for a life of mediocrity.
Ben Franklin said,
"Most people die at 30 but aren't buried until 70."
When existence becomes a way of life and
an end in itself, life ceases to be filled
with joy, passion and creative expression.

Trying

If there's one word I cannot bear,
We often say, too often hear,
A word dividing do from don't,
And is from isn't, will from won't,
A harmless word or so it seems,
Yet *trying* sabotages dreams.
Try equates with hesitate,
Like standing still or watch and wait.

The acrobat, he does not *try*;
Precision moves, it's do or die.
You might not like this cautious stand–
The pilot says he'll *try* to land.
If rescue workers were to say
I'll *try* to save your child today,
You might feel frightened, insecure,
Without commitment or something more.

If *try* is all that you can do
Then don't begin, it's not for you.
Do it poorly but don't *try*.
You might as well just tell a lie.
Make a promise that you'll do
Then forge ahead and follow through.
You'll like yourself when you don't *try*,
So bid that word a fast goodbye.

The Road to Talk

The road to talk is just a walk,
Intentions cheap to say.
The words are free and plentiful
And freely go away.

A name is built with confidence,
Responsiveness a must;
And doing what you say you'll do
Will earn you faith and trust.

A leader will not keep his lead
Without his follow-through
As people listen for his words
And watch what he will do.

Integrity becomes the price;
A reputation lost,
A name and claim to leadership
Is what becomes the cost.

The stakes are high, a heavy debt
May never be repaid,
If you go back upon your word,
A promise that you made.

Know that you deserve everything
you want and you can have it.
It will take commitment and hard work.
Part of the prize is the person
you will become in the process.

Crossroads

I've reached the crossroads of my life.
A choice has come my way:
To venture now from what I know–
Perhaps today's the day.

If only I had money saved,
My children on their own,
My bills were paid, the house repaired,
I didn't need a loan.

What if I should not succeed?
What will my family say?
The years you worked, you studied hard;
You're throwing that away?

If I should wait a year or two
Until I'm more secure,
This chance I have may pass me by
And leave no open door.

I can't erase these thoughts, this dream,
An urging not to wait.
I see my life in my control,
The master of my fate.

I can look for obstacles
And fear what isn't known.
Or I can choose to take a step
Outside my comfort zone.

Circumstances fading now,
I set my mind to win.
The turning point has come to pass;
Today I will begin.

Find it in your heart to forgive.
Let go of anger, hate,
resentment and expectations of others.
Know that the only person you can control is yourself.
Take charge of your thoughts, your deeds and your life.
Keep love in your heart at all times
and it will serve you well.

Where You've Come Before

Knowing yourself, the reason for your journey,
Pain is your friend, your teacher and your guide.
Choose how to feel and you'll create your future.
Looking outside your heart is not a place to hide.

Come take my hand, the hand of all your brothers.
Where you are now, and where you are to go,
Here where you walk along a lonely highway,
This is the road to truth, the peace you long to know.

Look at the stars; that's not where you'll find heaven,
Look at the sky; it's closer than your heart.
Look in my eyes, and there find your reflection
Where you have gone before is again where you may start.

Measure success by your own standards,
not by the standards of others.
Decide what success means to you
on the inside—not by what others tell you it is.
Dare to be different.

Success

A child is born to poverty with rags upon his back.
From nourishment to medicine, there always is a lack.
And in this ghetto where he grows, surrounded by despair,
He sees himself as prosperous through dreams and hope and prayer.

His optimistic attitude and will to be his best,
There's nothing that he cannot do when challenged to a test.
His ears are deaf to ridicule, their laughter and their sneers,
Like droplets falling off a duck, their words he cannot hear.

The sunshine streaming from his heart, his faith a guiding light;
While others grope within the dark, the paths he takes are bright.
The moving force within his soul, belief his only need,
A vision always in his sight that drives him to succeed.

Some believe success in life depends upon pure chance,
That destiny's beyond control–it cannot be enhanced.
Others know this isn't so, the truth revealed in dreams–
No limits but the ones we set, in spite of how it seems.

The gifts of Michelangelo, Ben Franklin and Thoreau
Are choices for humanity, where you and I may go.
Believe it and it is the truth, not just for rich and smart.
So stretch beyond your comfort zone, today's the day to start.

Embrace failure. It is through failure
that we learn, discover and grow.
With failure comes intense emotion—much stronger than
the emotion that comes with victory.
It is this intense emotion that propels us forward.
Every time you set out to do something and you fail,
ask yourself, "What can I learn from this experience?
What do these mistakes offer me?"
Next time you fail, think about people like Edison,
Lincoln, and Oprah Winfrey.
These courageous people failed over and over.
They knew the value of persistence,
of not giving up just because things didn't work out
the first time—or the tenth time.
Each failure offers a valuable lesson.
Embrace it, for it is your teacher.

The Puzzle

From dusk to dawn and back again, just any other day.
Like worker bees they're programmed to behave the same old way.
A picture puzzle is their world, each life a piece within.
And in a moment they're displaced, not fitting where they've been.

While some will force their way back in, they'll suffer strife and pain.
Existence marked by misery and nothing do they gain.
Always crying woe is me, they're in the victim seat,
Wanting only sympathy, content in their defeat.

Others facing challenges, no longer well aligned,
Their borders so irregular, distort the whole design.
And yet they do not force their way or dwell in deep despair,
Believing they must change themselves, courageously they dare.

A fortitude and will resides, implanted in their soul,
A dream so vivid it is real, directing every goal.
Failures act as obstacles, diversions on the way,
That test their faith from time to time, (but winners seldom stray).

The dream must be unshakable, no matter what the stakes.
To make the puzzle whole again, one must do what it takes.
Success is but an attitude that anyone can choose.
It's not about a game of chance where some will win and lose.

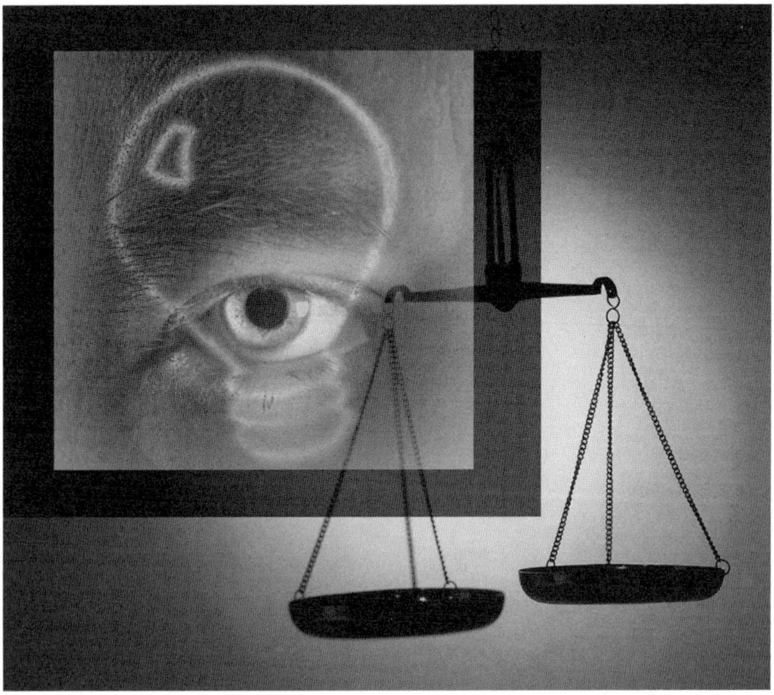

Decisions

At times I have to sort things out,
Decide which choice is better.
To my dismay my heart and head
Sometimes don't work together.
While part of me wants facts alone
That just support my vision,
Another part says trust your heart
And use your intuition.

Never listen to advice
Although it comes from caring,
Suggesting what is right for them,
For you it has no bearing.
So if you find you can't decide,
Don't let it bring you sorrow.
Just go have fun and be carefree;
There always is tomorrow.

Relationships

A True Friend

Once in a rare while, God opens the door for people to meet and become special friends. A true friend is a rare friend. He or she is someone who:

- Listens and seeks to understand.
- Sees your strengths when you see limitations.
- Picks you up and brightens your day when you need it the most.
- Can hear the sorrow in your heart even without your words.
- Believes that you can, even when you believe you cannot.
- Sees beyond your faults and helps you turn your liabilities into assets.
- Can feel your excitement, disappointments and challenges by just being present.
- Tells you the truth, even when it is hard to tell.
- Gives you hugs unconditionally.
- Is loyal and always on your team.
- Is compassionate, kind and caring.
- Is there for you when others are not.
- Shares your laughter, your tears, your successes, your failures.

A true friend is more precious than a rare gem. He or she is a gift from God and a blessing. You, my dear friend, are a blessing for me. You are my true friend.

May you always remember this moment and feel
the abundant love that flows through you, with you and to you.
I am blessed because of you—my true friend.

My Little Girl

Your little hands, your tiny feet,
I still remember when
You started as a part of me;
I was much younger then.
The sleepless nights I still recall,
You needed to be fed.
As tired and weary as I was,
I staggered from my bed.
And when you gazed into my eyes,
A smile with me you shared,
It touched my heart deep in my soul;
No sacrifice was spared.
The years passed by,
You grew and grew,
A reason for my being.
Your clever wit and loving ways
Were all that I was seeing.
A mother's love that binds her child
Is hard to understand,
For those who never walk that road,
Or never play that hand.
As for me I know for sure
Without the slightest doubt:
I'd never change a single thing.
You're what my life's about.

On Mother's Day

It wasn't very long ago you stroked my little head.
And wished for me upon a star, then tucked me in my bed,
Stories that you were to tell, they never did get old.
When you were just a little girl, those stories too were told.

It wasn't very long ago, at home, in school, at play,
Through each defeat and victory, you praised me anyway.
My mother, teacher, friend you were, in best and darkest hour.
You saw in me what I could not; you were my rock and power.

And when I dreamed outlandish dreams you told me they could be;
Dismissed the doubts that visited, saw more than I could see.
My time it came to leave the nest. It was my time to fly.
I wished that I could be like you, an eagle flying high.

It wasn't very long ago, and still it's true today.
Your love and strength inspired me; it's time for me to say.
On Mother's Day and every day I want for you to know.
You hold a place within my heart. I'll always love you so.

Grandmother

Though older and graying, she's giving and wise:
A grandmother's love always shows in her eyes.
From small tots to teens, they will come and they'll go;
Like blossoming flowers, she watches them grow.

Through multiplication they increase her pleasure,
Each grandchild a blessing, a keepsake and treasure.
Unconditional love for each one that she shows,
From the tops of their heads to the tips of their toes.

They love to hear stories that she loves to tell,
It's part of her job and she does it quite well.
She never gets tired of the answers to "why,"
Each comes with a hug and a wink of her eye.

It's almost by magic she makes dreams come true.
Instinctively grandmothers know what to do.
Indulges and spoils them, for they seldom stay;
It's a grandmother's privilege to do it this way.

Of their milestones and triumphs, she never will tire,
She inspires and empowers their will and desire.
Through their highs and their lows, she brings comfort and cheer,
Though a distance away, in her heart, always near.

A teacher, a friend, a compassionate soul,
She's the bridge in our history that makes us feel whole.
It's time to pay tribute, to honor, revere,
And let you know, Grandmother; we're glad you're here.

Dear Aunt

My aunt is like a flawless gem, she's valuable and rare.
She truly has a heart of gold; with everyone she'll share.
So kind and giving is my aunt, she's never cross or cruel,
She sees the good in every soul and yet she is no fool.

Her share of tragedies she's had; she's weathered many storms.
So cheerful is her attitude, an icy room she warms.
By years she's now advanced in life, just where she'd like to hold.
Her spirit will live on and on; she never will grow old.

From childhood memories I recall elation and delight.
The thought of my beloved aunt, a darkened world turned bright.
Never thinking of herself, with joy and love so free.
These qualities admired so, like her I wished to be.

If riches and prosperity are measured by how much
Others love and care for her, so many lives she's touched.
My aunt indeed is richer than the wealthiest by far.
She lights the lives that cross her path, just like the brightest star.

The words we wish to be expressed when days on earth are gone,
Is how we should conduct our lives the start of each new dawn.
My aunt can surely rest assured, her eulogy will read,
She left a mark, because of her a better world will be.

Too often life will pass us by, our love concealed in prayer.
And yet we do not say the words, so those we love can hear.
I'd like to say to you, dear aunt, I want for you to know,
You hold a special place for me. I'll always love you so.

Graduation Day

Today's the day we honor you, send love and blessings too.
Our prayers for you to know true joy through what you say and do.
Rejoice in your accomplishments, for you have come so far;
A milestone and a victory that's brought you where you are.
And as you hold your head up high, embrace that scroll in hand;
Just hold that vision of the joy, and honor where you stand.
For this exhilaration is the power that you'll find,
Propels and fuels the dreams you dream, the passions in your mind.
Those dreams can take you anywhere; believe that you can be
And settle not for getting by or mediocrity.
Enjoy and celebrate your day; remember as you go,
Your past and all your memories, the happiness you know.
Hold this treasure in your heart and walk with pride today.
Your road ahead has just begun, you'll soon be on your way.
A road that's filled with obstacles and opportunity:
Your choice to see what you will see, to be what you will be.
One door will close with scroll in hand, your gateway to begin,
With seeds to be a shining star whose time has come to win.

My Valentine

A ray of sun through curtains glows.
Another time from long ago
I find myself remembering when
My Valentine, you were back then.

The only love I was to know,
I felt the sting of Cupid's bow.
You light my life throughout all time,
And I am yours and you are mine.

Sometimes you seem to disappear;
A mere illusion, you're right here.
For I can feel you in my soul.
Within my heart you make me whole.

In the stillness of my mind,
Your love I know I'll always find.
It's meant to be. Your love's the sign,
My one and only Valentine.

Wedding Day

Ivory lace and baby's breath
With rosebuds in her hair;
A champagne toast and gourmet foods
With song and dance and cheer;

As he holds her in his arms
With passion burning bright,
The background fades,
They stand alone surrounded by a light.

This day begins a journey of a lifetime that they'll share.
Each promises undying love; in hard times too they'll care.
In silence he can hear her thoughts and she can hear his too.
A joy that words cannot express; their dreams will all come true.

They raise their glass and sip champagne and feel a glow within.
How blessed they are to share this day among their friends and kin.
With faith and prayer a lighted path will always show the way,
And passions fueled by memories of their special Wedding Day.

Restless Pastures

In restless pastures she wanders aimlessly in the darkness,
Blindly groping for the light, for peace and harmony,
For a melody soothing to her soul.
She longs for perfect union,
Coupling,
The fiery elation and ecstasy that comes
Only from the merger with a soul mate.
But locked is she,
A prisoner in bondage with chains that hold her back.
And she can choose to free herself,
To find purpose and passion,
And become master of her fate.
The decision has always been in her hands
In these restless pastures.

A Turning Point

Face to face she looks at him, directly in his eyes.
Her words don't come too easily, she tries hard not to cry.
"Once upon a time," she says, "a long, long time ago;
I had a dream of years to come, we loved each other so."

"The vows we took were promises to love till death us part,
But all that's left is emptiness where passions filled my heart.
So many years have long since passed, the flame it slowly died.
Perhaps we didn't care enough, the many times we tried."

A void is left within her heart, entangled with her soul;
A part of her has gone away; without it she's not whole.
She cannot change what he's become, the only thing she knows,
She'll change herself or walk away, or lower she will go.

A couple dances cheek to cheek, their passion and their fire
Is on display for all to see, their longing and desire.
A partner's gone, died long ago. She hears this tale of woe.
Their burning love will never fade. She'll always love him so.

She tells him this is what she wants; it's how she wants to feel.
Not fantasies or dreams she wished but never were made real.
Her loveless life is a mistake, a paradox she sees.
Like fish and water, birds and bees; together they must be.

Her final plea, she speaks the words and forces back her tears,
"Please take my hand and walk with me," He listens and he hears,
"Let's start again right here and now and leave the pain behind;
A chance for us to love again means making ties that bind."

Motherhood

The challenges of motherhood amaze me every day.
It seems I can do nothing right, no matter what I say.
The teenage years are difficult, the worst of which I'm told
Will age me far beyond my years, will make me gray and old.

The slightest little argument can set her off for sure.
From joy to rage and back again is what I must endure.
Although I try to keep her safe, she knows much more than me.
She's just a babe at age fifteen; she thinks she's twenty-three.

Her clothes are all the latest rage, the jeans she thinks are cool
Will be old news in record time; if worn, she'll be a fool.
Her friends cannot converse with me, I'm transportation queen,
I must pretend she's not with me in public if we're seen.

She cannot help her teenage ways that make her hard to bear.
She also has a gentle side, a sweetness so sincere.
The moments may be few and brief; at times we like each other.
And when she's sick, there is no doubt, she always wants her mother.

Her special charm, her clever wit that makes me love her so,
It picks my spirits up so high when I am feeling low.
She is the light that lights my life, it's plainly clear to see.
It matters not how tough it gets; her mother I will be.

Make a Difference

Make a difference
For someone
On each and every day.
Forgive the past,
Show gratitude,
Make giving be your way.

Some caring words,
A kindness shown,
An intimate embrace;
These warm the heart
And feed the soul,
A tranquil happy place.

A gentle touch,
A friendly smile,
An empathetic ear;
Collectively
They multiple,
Transforming sad to cheer.

Make a difference
For someone
And let your light shine through.
Before your eyes
You'll be surprised
As others follow you.

My Angel

At a time of my life filled with strife and despair,
She came into my world as an answer to prayer.
Blue-eyed and blond hair with a confident style,
Refined and exquisite her manner and smile.

I didn't know how and I didn't know why
She exuded success; this I couldn't deny.
Her manner uplifting with never a doubt,
A fear or concern, that she once spoke about.

Enlightened with purpose, with goals and desire,
She awakened my spirit and set me on fire.
I followed her lead, she inspired me so.
On prosperity's path we together would go.

An angel indeed, in her spirit and soul,
With halo and wings, you could see their soft glow.
An angel, my angel, just look and you'll see:
She's holding a candle for you and for me.

about Ruth Kuttler,

the poet, author and graphic artist

I was born in Washington, DC and spent most of my life in Maryland working as a clinical nurse and nursing instructor. After receiving Bachelor of Science and Master of Science degrees in nursing from the University of Maryland, I completed postmasters training and certification as a nurse practitioner in family medicine. Although I was an award-winning writer academically, I never even attempted to write creatively or just for fun.

One day my world was turned upside down when I found myself without a job. For the first time ever, I started to question my purpose. The thought of working in my profession for many more years filled me with a sense of dread. I started to pay attention to those feelings. Just by chance, I happened upon a poetry contest and decided to enter. My poem, titled "Going Not Where I Know," was published in an anthology. What was more important was the emergence of a gift and passion for writing poetry. I decided to let go of nursing and follow my heart. It led me to develop my talents as a writer, graphic artist, web designer and marketing consultant. Although this gave me great satisfaction, it didn't satisfy my burning desire to share my poetry and art. Eventually I came to understand that Visions in Verse is my true purpose and passion. My mission is to share it and make it an important part of who I am. I love what I do every day. It doesn't even feel like work. That's all part of God's great plan.

(continued on page 86)

Today, I am an accomplished poet and graphic artist. My poetry has been published many times in newspapers, magazines and hard-bound poetry anthologies. Two of my poems were selected among thousands to be recorded on DVDs and record collections produced by the International Society of Poetry. I have received editor's choice awards and I'm recognized in the International Who's Who of Poetry. In addition to being a published poet with my own book, I am an award-winning speaker with repeated invitations to display my work and present my poetry to groups at local libraries and organizations in my community.

I believe my poetry is my own little pipeline to God, expressed as poetic verses with a message to think and follow your heart. Much of my poetry and art is about conveying the message that we should live our passions. If it feels good and right, then do it; if it doesn't, make a decision to change. We all have genius within us. It's not just in some of us or just for the rich or smart. If you learn to listen and open your mind, God will provide the answers. Of course, you have to do something different if you want different results.

I hope you enjoy these poems. They are gifts from my heart to yours. Share them with the ones you love. It's one of the best gifts you can give.

How to Order

Order one or many copies of Visions in Verse™–this one-of-a-kind collection–and give them as gifts for loved ones or special friends. People enjoy these heartfelt poems, quotes and stories in verse, and love to read them over and over–poems with a message that inspire, empower and make people think about possibilities. This beautifully illustrated collection will keep on giving, renewing feelings of joy and hope.

See the following Visions in Verse™ products at www.VisionsinVerse.com:

8" x 10" framed collection to personalize with your picture (easel-backed)

Wedding Day

Graduation Day

Opening Doors

11" x 14" framed themed collection (wall mount)

A True Friend

Dear Aunt

On Mother's Day

My Little Girl

Grandmother

Graduation Day

Wedding Day

Eternal Love

My Valentine

Opening Doors

The Best Christmas Gift

The Rose

For more information and to order online, please visit www.VisionsinVerse.com or send an email to ruth@VisionsinVerse.com.

To inquire about wholesale orders for stores or volume discounts, call our toll-free number.

For retail or wholesale orders, call toll-free (orders only):
1-800- 319-0234